MOTORCYCLES

Story and photos by Andy Belcher

Contents

CAMBRIDGE UNIVERSITY PRESS

UCL Institute of Education

EARLY MOTORCYCLES

Millions of people all over the world ride motorcycles.

They have changed a lot since the first one was built in 1867.

Motorcycles have become bigger, stronger and more comfortable.

*Early motorcycles looked more like a bicycle with an **engine**.*

*This motorcycle, built in 1931, had a big **fuel tank**, a strong frame, strong wheels and a large padded seat.*

MOTORCYCLES TODAY

Today, there are lots of different motorcycles. Some are colourful, some are fast and some are big.

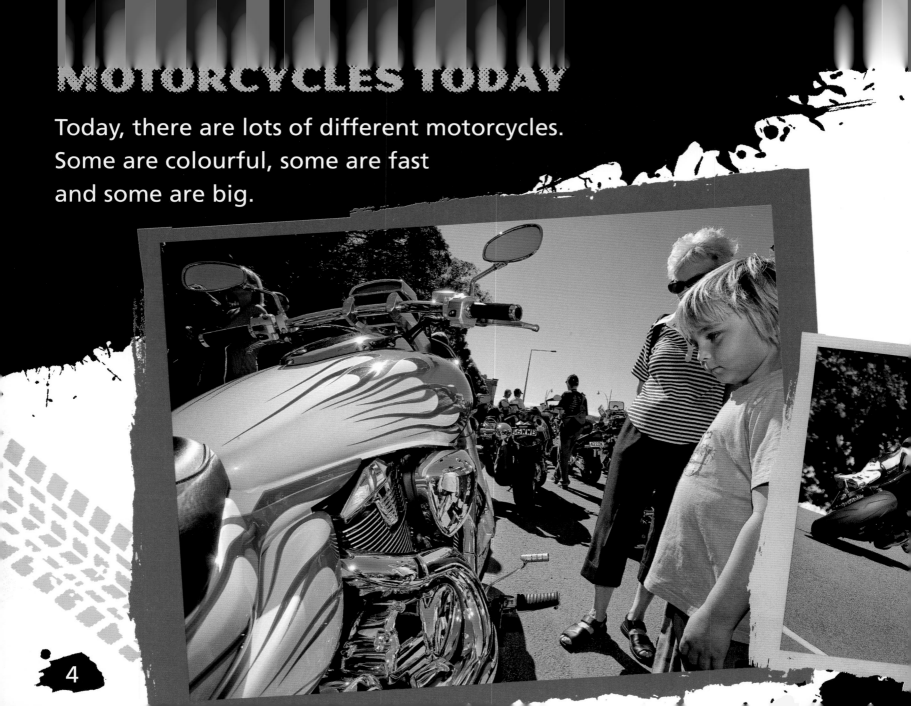

Riders need to wear helmets for safety.

Motorcycling is very popular, but it can be **dangerous**.

Today, motorcycles are built with similar parts.

pillion passenger

fuel tank

fairing

seating for rider and passenger

mud guard

engine

luggage box

front forks

exhaust muffler

Touring motorcycles are designed to carry two people with plenty of luggage. The motorcycles can go on different types of road.

This Suzuki off road touring motorcycle can take a passenger.

POWERFUL MOTORCYCLES

Some motorcycles are designed to be very fast and powerful.

◄◄ *This engine is bigger than the engine of a small car.*

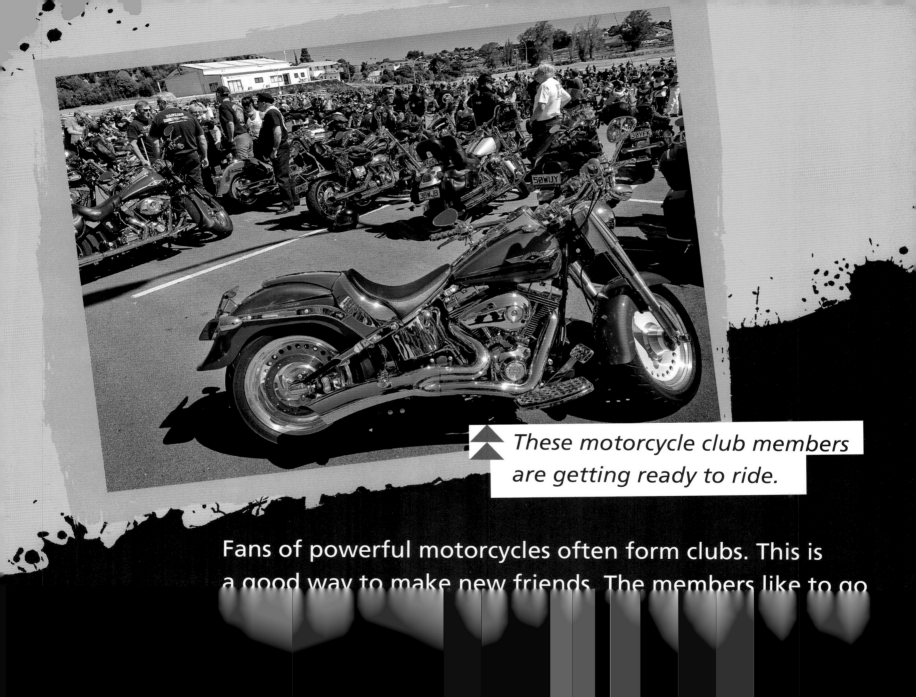

These motorcycle club members are getting ready to ride.

Fans of powerful motorcycles often form clubs. This is a good way to make new friends. The members like to go

MOTORCYCLES IN THE CITY

Scooters are small motorcycles with small engines.
They are easy to ride and good for short city trips.

These scooter riders are waiting in heavy traffic.

an electric moped

Mopeds are smaller than scooters. They have pedals like a bicycle. A new type of moped is powered by electricity. Its **battery** needs charging every night. This moped does not pollute the air, because it has no petrol engine and no exhaust pipe.

Tuk-tuks are three-wheeled motorcycles. In many cities tuk-tuks are used as taxis. Passengers pay the driver a **fare** to get a ride.

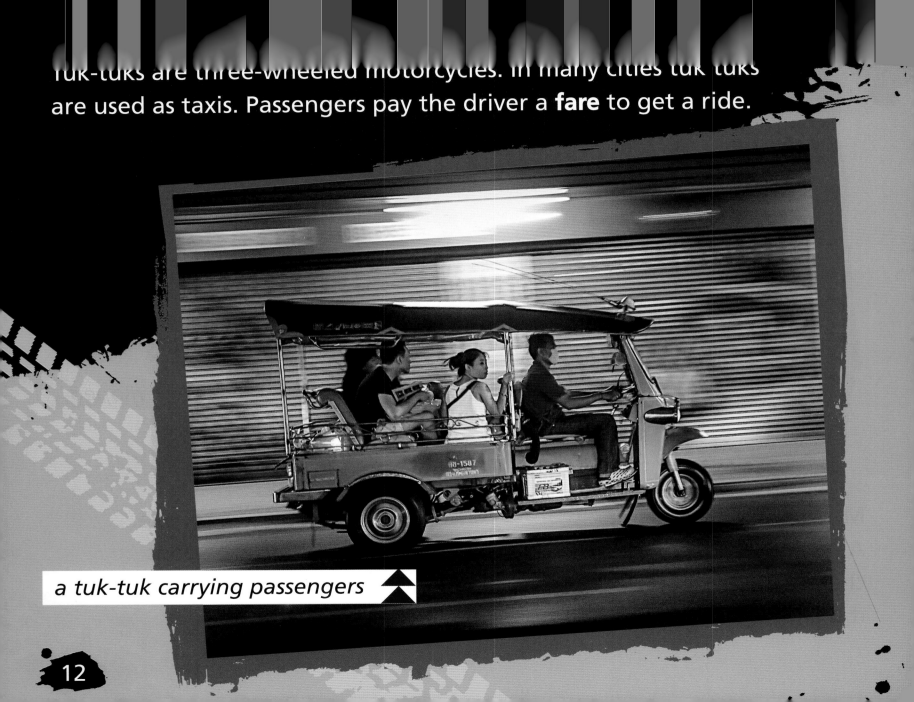

a tuk-tuk carrying passengers

Larger motorcycles can be used in the city and on the open road, too.

UNUSUAL MOTORCYCLES

Sometimes, **mechanics** adapt or rebuild motorcycles into unusual designs. They add bigger engines, new seats, longer **handlebars** and even **sidecars** to carry another person.

This motorcycle has very long forks which hold the wheel far out in front. This style of motorcycle is called a 'chopper'.

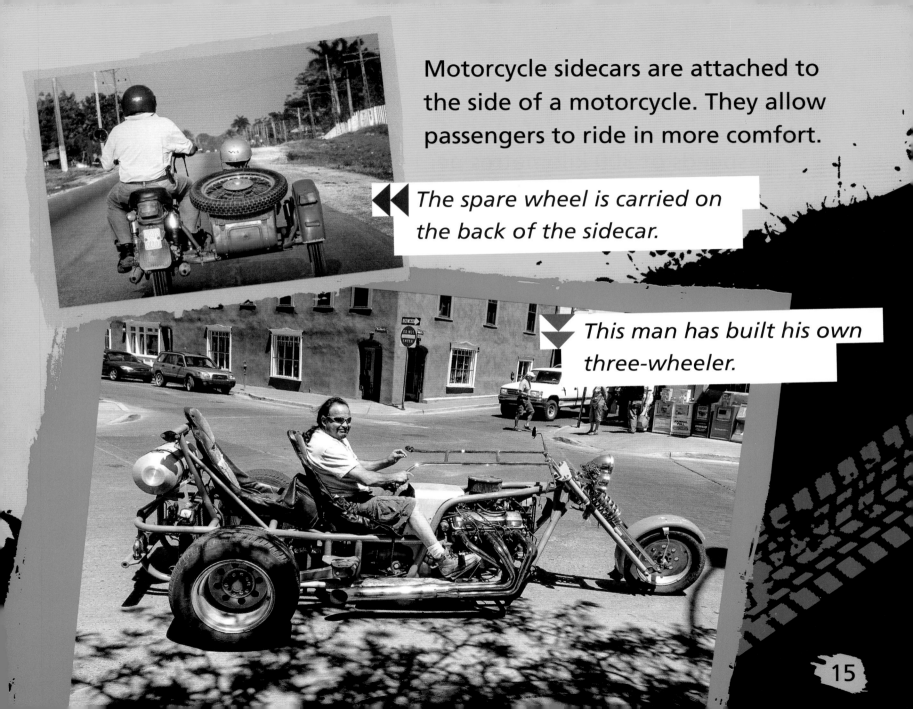

Motorcycle sidecars are attached to the side of a motorcycle. They allow passengers to ride in more comfort.

The spare wheel is carried on the back of the sidecar.

This man has built his own three-wheeler.

MOTORCYCLE RACING

Motorcycle racing is a popular sport all over the world. Motorcycle racers can reach speeds of 300 kilometres per hour. The bikes lean over so far in the bends that the rider's knee often touches the **tarmac**. His leather suit has special plastic **kneepads** so he won't hurt his knee.

Many people come to watch the race.

Some people race old motorcycles with a sidecar attached. The passenger on the sidecar is called a swinger. To stop the bike tipping over, the swinger must lean into the corners. The rider and swinger wear full leather suits to protect themselves in case they fall off.

Drag racing motorcycles race on a straight track. The rider will try to cross the finish line as quickly as possible.

This drag bike accelerates quickly.

Another type of motorcycle sport is called **motocross**. Here, riders race specially **adapted** motorcycles around several laps of a muddy track. The winner is the first to complete the course.

When the race starts, the bikes are very close to each other.

Motocross riders wear brightly, coloured safety gear.

SAFETY

Riding a motorcycle can be dangerous. Riders need good safety gear, for example, a helmet and leather suit with kneepads. Riding with the **headlight** on means car drivers can see you more easily in the dark and also during the day.

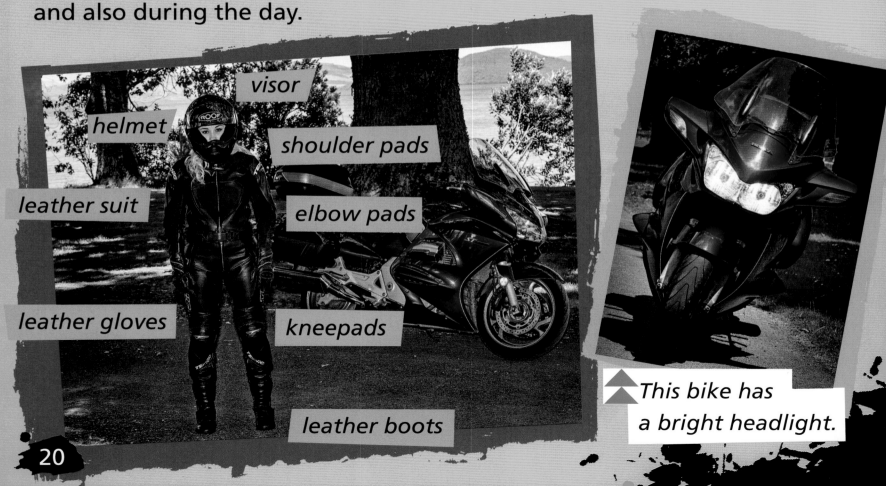

visor

helmet

shoulder pads

leather suit

elbow pads

leather gloves

kneepads

leather boots

This bike has a bright headlight.

Motocross riders also need good safety gear. This rider has just finished a race. She is wearing a **neck brace** in case she falls off.

◀◀ *motocross safety gear*

◀◀ *This young rider was sprayed with mud. The goggles keep mud out of your eyes.*

It is really important to wear a good helmet

GLOSSARY

adapted changed

battery object that provides electricity

dangerous unsafe

engine part of a vehicle that uses energy to make it move

fare money you pay to travel

fuel tank container that holds petrol and other fuel

handlebars part of a vehicle that you hold onto to control direction

headlight main light at the front of the motorcycle

helmet hard hat that protects the wearer's head and face

kneepads hard flat pads that are worn on the knees to protect them

mechanics people whose job is to repair machines

motocross sport of racing over rough ground on special motorcycles

neck brace stiff collar worn to protect the neck

sidecars small one-wheeled vehicle attached to the side of a motorcycle

tarmac thick, black substance that becomes very hard and is used to cover roads

INDEX

MOTORCYLES  Andy Belcher

Teaching notes written by Sue Bodman and Glen Franklin

Using this book

Developing reading comprehension

This challenging non-fiction report is written in the present tense. Many specific and technical terms are used. A thorough introduction covering the important terms and parts of the motorcycle will be needed before reading. Labelled diagrams provide clear graphics to support learning how to read for information effectively.

Grammar and sentence structure

- Sentences follow the language features of the genre style (for example, present tense, language structures showing the focus on generic groups, for example, *'Motorcycles have ...'*; *'Motorcycles can ...'*).
- Different punctuation styles used for labels and captions.
- Text is grouped into topics, typical in a non-chronological report.

Word meaning and spelling

- Decoding multisyllabic technical terms that are likely to be novel to the young reader (*'chopper'*, *'sidecar'*, *'tarmac'*, *'motocross'*, *'mechanics'*).
- Reading and spelling topic words, using the glossary to find out their meaning.

Curriculum links

Science - Children could label other transport and riders/drivers in the same style as pages 6 and 20.

History - Discuss other modes of transport, comparing early versions and contemporary versions (bicycles, buses and aeroplanes, for example). Support the discussion with photographs. This could lead to writing activities to draw comparisons between the two examples.

Learning Outcomes

Children can:

- locate information in the text which supports their comprehension
- use labelled diagrams to develop understanding
- problem-solve new topic words that are not completely decodable.

A guided reading lesson

Book Introduction

Give each child a copy of the book. Ask them to read the title and blurb quietly to themselves.

Orientation

Ask the children what type of text they think this is. Establish that the book is a report about motorcycles. Ask: *What do we already know about motorcycles?* Draw out prior knowledge and as a group formulate some questions about motorcycles that the children would like to explore as they read. You might want to record these questions on a whiteboard or flipchart so that the children can refer to it as they read.

Preparation

Pages 2 and 3: Look at the pictures of early motorbikes and using the photographs, labels and captions ask the children to suggest aspects that have changed.

Pages 4, 5, 6 and 7: Review the children's suggestions and add in aspects that they didn't name.

Page 5: Focus on the word *'dangerous'*. Read it aloud, asking the children to put their finger under the word as you say it. Say: *Let's find out what 'dangerous' means. Where will you look? Remember a glossary is in alphabetical order. Found it? Now you've read the definition, can you tell me what 'dangerous' means?*

Page 20: Look at the clothing that motorcycle riders should wear. Read the words as a group and suggest reasons that each piece of clothing is needed.

Strategy Check

There are some words that might be new to you in this book. Remember what you can do to read new words. Rehearse strategies such as reading through the word to blend the sounds; looking for known 'chunks' within new words; thinking about what would make sense and checking the glossary.